Snap
books®

Horse
BREEDS

CLYDESDALE HORSES

by John Diedrich

CAPSTONE PRESS
a capstone imprint

Snap Books are published by Capstone Press,
1710 Roe Crest Drive, North Mankato, Minnesota 56003
www.mycapstone.com

Library of Congress Cataloging-in-Publication Data
Names: Diedrich, John, author. Title: Clydesdale horses / by John
Diedrich. Description: North Mankato, Minnesota : Capstone Press, [2018]
| Series: Snap books. Horse breeds | Audience: Age 8-14. | Includes
bibliographical references and index. Identifiers: LCCN 2017038721 (print)
| LCCN 2017048697 (ebook) | ISBN 9781543500486 (eBook PDF) | ISBN
9781543500363 (hardcover) | ISBN 9781543500424 (pbk.) Subjects:
LCSH: Clydesdale horse--Juvenile literature. | Horse breeds--Juvenile
literature. Classification: LCC SF293.C65 (ebook) | LCC SF293.C65 D542
2018 (print) | DDC 636.1/5--dc23 LC record available at https://lccn.loc.
gov/2017038721"

Editorial Credits
Amy Kortuem, editor
Kayla Rossow, designer
Morgan Walters, media researcher
Kathy McColley, production specialist

Image Credits
Alamy: Findlay, 15; Getty Images: Holly Hildreth, 22; iStockphoto:
Gannet77, 23; Shutterstock: 1000 Words, 6, 42beats, Cover,
blue67design, (floral sketch) design element throughout, Christopher
Halloran, 1, 27, gvictoria, 19, johnbraid, 5, 8, Juliata, (floral) design
element throughout, L. Kramer, (fish scale) design throughout, Margo
Harrison, 20, 21, Muskoka Stock Photos, 14, Nicole Ciscato, 13, Olga_i,
12, Paul McKinnon, 11, paulista, 2, 3, redstone, (paper background)
design element throughout, suns07butterfly, (watercolor) design element
throughout, yod67, (horse vector) design element; SuperStock: Juniors,
16, 17, 25, 29

Printed and bound in the United States.
042718 000438

TABLE OF CONTENTS

Chapter 1

Willing Workers

The Clydesdale is one of the most familiar horse breeds. Most people have seen Clydesdales in TV commercials, movies, and magazines.

The Clydesdale belongs to a group called draft horses. These strong horses were first bred to work on farms and to pull large loads in cities. They are still used for these purposes in some parts of the world.

Beginning of the Breed

The Clydesdale breed began in the early 1700s in a part of Scotland called Lanarkshire. Lanarkshire is near the large city of Glasgow.

Clydesdales are draft horses.
They were first bred for farm work
and to pull carts and wagons.

Glasgow was near coalfields. The coal workers needed strong horses to pull the heavy coal wagons. As Scotland's cities grew, so did the need for coal. The coal workers needed stronger and faster horses to keep up with the demand.

Some people still use Clydesdales for farm work.

Around 1720 a Lanarkshire farmer named John Patterson bought a large black Flemish **stallion** in England. He bred the stallion to the smaller Scottish **mares**. The mares' foals were the earliest ancestors of today's Clydesdales.

Lanarkshire farmers continued to breed the large horses. Over time the farmers produced a powerful horse with a long stride. Farmers hitched the horses to plows to work their fields. The farmers called the horses Clydesdales. Lanarkshire is in the dale, or valley, of the Clyde River.

WORLD TRAVELERS

In 1826 Clydesdale owners showed off their horses at a world's fair called the Glasgow Exhibition. There, people from around the world saw Clydesdales for the first time.

Word spread about the big Scottish draft horses. People from other countries came to Scotland to buy Clydesdales. The new owners took the horses back to their own countries.

stallion—an adult male horse that can be used for breeding
mare—an adult female horse

By the late 1800s the Clydesdale breed had spread to North America. Clydesdales were used for farm work and to pull large loads in cities. In 1910 about 16,000 Clydesdales lived in the United States.

Today Clydesdales often pull wagons at parades and festivals.

YEARS OF DECLINE

By the 1930s people needed fewer horses for work. Farmers replaced horses with tractors and other farm machines. Cars replaced horse-drawn carriages and wagons.

Clydesdale numbers decreased for the next 30 years. The breed was in danger of dying out.

RECENT YEARS

In the 1960s more people began raising Clydesdales. This time the horses were bred as show horses as well as for farm work. More Clydesdale shows and sales were held as people became interested in the big, gentle horses.

The Clydesdale Breeders of the U.S.A. keeps track of each U.S. Clydesdale's ancestry. This group formed in 1879. It now registers more than 500 new horses each year.

FACT

A horseshoe for a Clydesdale is around 12 inches (30.48 centimeters) long, or the size of a dinner plate. Each one weighs 5 pounds (2.27 kilograms). You can fit four Thoroughbred horseshoes inside just one Clydesdale horseshoe.

Chapter 2
Gentle Giants

Clydesdales are born big. A newborn Clydesdale foal weighs about 125 to 150 pounds (57 to 68 kg).

A horse's height is measured in hands. A hand equals 4 inches (10 cm). An adult Arabian horse is 14 to 15 hands tall at the **withers**. The average Clydesdale reaches this height by its first birthday.

Most Clydesdales reach their full height of 16 to 19 hands by age 3 or 4. Adult Clydesdales weigh between 1,600 and 2,300 pounds (725 and 1,050 kg). They are as heavy as small cars.

withers—the top of a horse's shoulders; a horse's height is measured from the ground to the withers

FACT

According to Guinness World Records, the world's tallest living horse was once a Clydesdale. Remington, a 3,000-pound (1,360-kg) Clydesdale from Texas, held this record. Remington measures 20 hands, or 80 inches (203.2 cm) tall. A Belgian horse took the title in 2010.

A foal can gain up to 4 pounds (1.8 kg) a day while still drinking its mother's milk.

FEATURES

The Clydesdale has more refined features than most draft breeds. Clydesdales have longer legs and more streamlined bodies. They also have a high-stepping trot.

Most Clydesdales have white markings.

The Clydesdale's lower legs are covered in long, silky hair called feather. The feather flows in the air as the Clydesdale trots.

The Clydesdale's hooves are larger than those of most other breeds. Each hoof is about the size of a large dinner plate.

COLOR

Clydesdales can be one of several colors. Bay is the most common color pattern. Bay horses are red-brown with a black mane and tail. Clydesdales can also be brown, black, chestnut, or roan. Chestnut is a shade of copper or red. Roan Clydesdales have coats of one solid color mixed with white hairs.

Most Clydesdales have white markings. A Clydesdale may have a white stripe called a blaze on its face. If the whole face is white, it is called a bald face. White markings on the lower legs are called socks or stockings. Some Clydesdales have white patches on their bodies.

PERSONALITY

Clydesdales are gentle and cooperative. They work hard and seem to want to please their owners. Their personalities make them easy to train.

Gentleness and cooperation are good characteristics for any horse. They are especially important for the big, powerful Clydesdale. A 2,000-pound (900-kg) horse with poor manners could be dangerous to people and other horses.

Clydesdales' gentle, cooperative personalities make them good show horses for young people.

bald face

wide nostrils

deep, wide chest

feather

white stockings

withers

short, broad back

long hind legs

Chapter 3
Champions in Harness

Today few Clydesdales are used for farm work. But many owners still train their Clydesdales to pull wagons. A Clydesdale can pull a wagon alone or with a team of horses.

LEARNING TO PULL

People start training their Clydesdales to pull wagons when the horses are about 2 years old. The trainer uses a **harness** and **bridle** to train the Clydesdale. The harness connects the horse to the wagon. The bridle holds a metal piece called a bit in the horse's mouth. The bit is attached to the lines. The driver uses the lines to steer.

harness—a set of straps and metal pieces that connect a horse to a plow, cart, or wagon

bridle—the straps that fit around a horse's head and connect to a bit to control a horse

The driver holds onto the lines to steer Clydesdales.

Clydesdales wear harnesses during hitch competitions.

Soon the young Clydesdale becomes used to the harness and bridle. The trainer hitches the young horse with an older, well-trained horse. The older horse pulls the young horse in the direction that the trainer is steering them.

A Winning Team

Hitches are teams of two, three, four, six, or eight horses harnessed together. Clydesdale hitches are usually made up of horses that are the same size and color. The horses trot together smoothly as they respond to the driver's commands.

Hitch competitions have different classes for the different sizes of hitches. Teams are judged on how well they work together. A good team and trainer make driving look easy. A team must start and stop when asked. It also should steer easily and turn smoothly.

MAJOR COMPETITIONS

The biggest Clydesdale show in the United States is the National Show. This three-day event includes breed, cart, hitch, riding, and **halter** classes.

halter—a rope or strap used to lead a horse; the halter fits over the horse's nose and behind its ears

Breed competitions are like beauty or fitness contests. Horses show against other Clydesdales of the same sex and age. The horse that best represents the breed wins.

In halter classes horses aren't ridden or hitched to a harness. Instead owners use a halter to lead the horses on foot.

Many state fairs and county fairs hold draft horse shows that include classes for Clydesdales. Young 4-H members often show their Clydesdales at these events. 4-H is an organization that teaches young people about leadership and community service.

Clydesdales win ribbons at competitions.

Chapter 4
Clydesdales in Action

Like all horses, Clydesdales need plenty of room. Many Clydesdale owners live in the country and keep their horses in barns on their property. Clydesdale owners who live in cities pay to board their horses at nearby farms or stables.

Draft horses eat about twice as much as smaller horses eat. Adult Clydesdales need 25 to 50 pounds (11 to 23 kg) of hay each day. They also eat about 5 to 10 pounds (2 to 5 kg) of concentrated feed daily. This food is made up of grain, vitamins, minerals, and molasses.

Clydesdales need plenty of space to exercise.

OTHER USES

Clydesdale horses are best known for harness and team competitions. But they also make good riding horses. Many people use Clydesdales for trail riding, jumping events, and **dressage** competitions. In dressage events, horses complete a pattern as they perform a series of advanced moves.

Some people use Clydesdales in **hippotherapy** programs. Hippotherapy uses riding to treat people who have disabilities. For example, a person who is unable to walk can feel the horse's movements during a ride. Riders can imitate these movements as they try to walk on their own. Clydesdales' calm, hardworking personalities make them good choices for these programs.

Clydesdales are also used for other jobs. They pull carriages at weddings and parades. A few people use them to pull logs in forests.

Clydesdales attract attention wherever they go. These gentle giants continue to amaze people with their strength, beauty, and friendly nature.

dressage—a riding style in which horses complete a pattern while doing advanced moves
hippotherapy—a treatment that uses horseback riding to help people with disabilities

Anheuser-Busch Clydesdales

The Anheuser-Busch Company has been famous for its Clydesdale teams since 1933. Today the company owns about 250 Clydesdales – one of the largest herds in the world.

To be on a Budweiser team a Clydesdale must meet strict standards. It has to be a bay **gelding**, be at least 4 years old, and stand 18 hands high. It must have four white stockings, a white blaze on the face, and a black mane and tail.

Each Clydesdale team makes hundreds of appearances across the country. It travels about 10 months of the year. Expert handlers, groomers, caretakers, and drivers travel with each team. When they're not traveling, the horses live on farms in Missouri, Colorado, and New Hampshire.

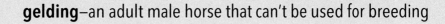

gelding–an adult male horse that can't be used for breeding

Fast Facts:
The Clydesdale Horse

Name: The Clydesdale breed's name comes from the dale, or valley, of the Clyde River in Scotland. Clydesdales were first bred in this valley.

History: The Clydesdale breed began in Scotland in the early 1700s. Flemish stallions were bred to Scottish draft mares.

Height: Clydesdales are 16 to 19 hands (about 6 feet or 1.8 meters) at the withers. Each hand equals 4 inches (10 centimeters).

Weight: 1,600 to 2,300 pounds (725 to 1,050 kilograms)

Colors: bay, brown, black, chestnut, roan

Features: wide foreheads; large eyes; feather on the legs; long stride; high-stepping trot

Abilities: Besides pulling carts and wagons, Clydesdales do well as show horses and in hippotherapy programs. Many people also use them for trail riding, jumping, and dressage.

Personality: gentle, cooperative, hardworking

Life span: 20 to 25 years

Glossary

bridle (BRYE-duhl)—the straps that fit around a horse's head and connect to a bit to control a horse while riding

dressage (druh-SAHJ)—a riding style in which horses complete a pattern while doing advanced moves

gelding (GEL-ding)—an adult male horse that can't be used for breeding

halter (HAWL-tur)—a rope or strap used to lead a horse; the halter fits over the horse's nose and behind its ears.

harness (HAR-niss)—a set of straps and metal pieces that connect a horse to a plow, cart, or wagon

hippotherapy (hip-oh-THAIR-uh-pee)—a treatment that uses horseback riding to help people with disabilities

mare (MAIR)—an adult female horse

stallion (STAL-yuhn)—an adult male horse that can be used for breeding

withers (WITH-urs)—the top of a horse's shoulders; a horse's height is measured from the ground to the withers

Read More

Dell, Pamela. *Clydesdales.* Majestic Horses. North Mankato, Minn.: Child's World, Inc., 2014.

Graubart, Norman. *Horses in American History.* How Animals Shaped History. New York: PowerKids Press, 2015.

Kolpin, Molly. *Favorite Horses: Breeds Girls Love.* Crazy About Horses. Mankato, Minn.: Capstone Press, 2015.

Internet Sites

Use FactHound to find Internet sites related to this book.

Visit *www.facthound.com*

Just type in 9781543500363 and go.

Check out projects, games and lots more at **www.capstonekids.com**

Index